California

Stephanie Lowman has been sketching and painting for over thirty years. Bringing to life past and present scenes from California was one of her most challenging projects. Stephanie studied fossils of prehistoric creatures and compared them to fossils of living animals to learn how they might have looked. She then spent countless hours drawing all of the animals and people line-by-line.

Stephanie currently lives in Arvada, Colorado, with her children, Osiris the Dog and Cassidy the Cat. She is also the illustrator of the books "Dreaming of Colorado," "Dreaming of Arches National Park," and "Dreaming of Rocky Mountain National Park."

Grant Collier has been working as a photographer and writer since 1996 and is the author of 15 books. Grant spent many months photographing in California to capture the images for this book. He also traveled to the crystal-clear waters of Aitutaki lagoon to shoot the over/under water scenes. If he couldn't get the image he needed, Grant used a tablet to draw parts of the landscape, including trees, light beams, and a kelp forest.

Grant carefully blended Stephanie's artwork into his images. He adjusted the lighting and shadows on the people and animals to match the lighting in the photographs.

©2020 Collier Publishing LLC ~ Text ©2020 Grant Collier ~ Illustrations ©2020 Stephanie Lowman & Grant Collier
All illustrations of living creatures by Stephanie Lowman ~ Background photos and landscape illustrations by Grant Collier

Book Design by Grant Collier
ISBN # 978-1-935694-50-2
Printed in South Korea

Published by Collier Publishing LLC ~ https://www.collierpublishing.com

This book may not be reproduced in full or in part by any means (with the exception of short quotes for purpose of review) without permission of the publisher.

Dreaming of California

Grant Collier ~ Stephanie Lowman

Collier Publishing LLC

Arvada, CO

Pandora the Pelican did not want to go to bed.
She wanted to swim with the seabirds instead.

She wanted to look into the turtle's eyes.
She wanted to hear the sea lion's cries.

She wanted to watch the dolphins play.
She wanted to see the eagle rays.

She wanted to dive into the ocean blue.
She wanted to see the sailfish too.

But her mom said she must get a good night's rest,
So Pandora had to fly back to her nest.

She lay down beside a beautiful tree,
And soon was dreaming of an age-old sea.

In her dream, an ancient world appeared.
It was wondrous, wild, and a little weird.

Inside, there were charming fish swimming near the shore,
And small animals living on the ocean floor.

But it was the marine reptiles who ruled this primal sea.
When they came near, even the bravest of fish would flee.

Supreme among these creatures were the mighty Shonisaurs.
They were larger than any beast that had ever lived before.

During this time, California was much hotter,
And most of its land was underwater.

To the east, there was a boundless land that was called Pangea.
To the west, the sea stretched out of sight, well beyond Korea.

Pandora soared over these waters without any fear,
Until she discovered another bright sphere.

Within this new world, she saw a saber-toothed cat,
Along with a heron and a cute, little bat.

Pandora flew below the huge granite peaks,
And saw more animals along a wide creek.

*Some of the creatures looked familiar,
But others were rather peculiar.*

The bison had horns that were far too long,
And the sloth was massive and much too strong.

Pandora realized she was still in the past.
She was lonely, stressed, and tiring fast.

*But then another glowing world appeared,
Which led to a forest that Pandora revered.*

Among the tall trees, she found many of her friends,
Including an owl, a jay, and a little wren.

The only humans here were like none she'd seen before.
They were Yurok Indians, who lived in the days of yore.

They built impressive houses out of nearby trees,
And made deerskin clothes so that they would not freeze.

The women wove baskets to carry water and food,
And the children played stick games to lighten the mood.

The men built canoes with great expertise,
So they could travel along rivers and seas.

They gathered together to
do a great tribal dance.

They wore their best outfits
and sang hypnotic chants.

Pandora was glad to see a great tribe of the West,

But she still wanted to get back to her nest.

*So she flew to another magic sphere,
That might take her back to the present year.*

The new land she found looked rather strange,
With a long winding river beneath an old mountain range.

Down by the stream, a man had just found some gold.
His name was James Marshall, or so the story was told.

James was a carpenter who was just building a mill.
He would never get rich. Mining wasn't his skill.

News of his find soon spread through the nation,
And people started heading west with elation.

If they hoped to strike gold, it was now or never,
But this mad rush of people would change California forever.

New roads were built and new cities created,
As the old way of life became outdated.

Now millions of people reside in this state,
Where ancient sea creatures once lived out their fate.

Suddenly, the images in Pandora's dream,
Began to fade and lose their gleam.

She woke from her slumber and opened her eyes,
Rejoicing in a glorious sunrise.

She told her mom in the early dawn,
About her dream of days long gone.

Pandora now knew that her mom was right.
You should get to sleep once day becomes night.

A rested mind and peaceful soul are more important than they seem.

Those who dare to do great things must sometimes stop and dream.

Did you know?

- 220 million years ago, during a period known as the Triassic, most of California was covered by an ocean.
- This ocean was filled with fish, lobsters, squid-like creatures, and large, ancient reptiles.
- The eastern part of California was part of a supercontinent called Pangea, which contained most of the land on Earth.
- During this time, California was located near the equator, so it was very hot.

- Beginning around 2.7 million years ago, a series of ice ages covered California's mountains with massive glaciers.
- As these glaciers slowly moved, they carved out the incredible granite rock formations seen in Yosemite National Park today.
- During this time, huge mammals, including the saber-toothed cat, long-horned bison, and giant sloth, roamed the land.
- Countless other animals that still exist today also lived among these giant beasts.
- In this book, Yosemite is pictured as it might have looked 35,000 years ago, in between two glacial maximums.

- Native American tribes have lived in California for well over 10,000 years.
- One such tribe is the Yurok, which has lived in the giant redwood forests of northern California for hundreds of years.
- The Yurok lived in large houses built out of cedar or redwood trees.
- They made dugout canoes from the trees and used them to travel up the Klamath river or along the coast.
- For food, the Yurok men caught fish and mollusks, and the women collected berries, acorns, seaweed, and roots.

- In 1847, James Marshall began building a mill in Coloma, California, for a man named John Sutter.
- In January of 1848, Marshall discovered flecks of gold in the American River near the mill.
- Word of Marshall's find soon spread throughout the world.
- In 1849, nearly 100,000 people, who were called the 49ers, came to California in search of gold.
- Many of the 49ers moved to San Francisco, which grow from a tiny community to a town with 36,000 people by 1852.

- The population of California has continued growing at a rapid rate for the past 170 years.
- Many huge cities have been built, including Los Angeles, which is now the second-largest city in the United States.
- Today, approximately 40 million people live in California, making it the most populous state in the nation.

Can you find the animals?

- While awake, Pandora saw a lot of animals living in and around the ocean. Can you find at least one of each of the following animals in the book? **Dolphin, harbor seal, humpback whale, sea otter, sea lion, bat ray (a type of eagle ray), jellyfish, leopard shark, sea turtle, wolf eel, bluefin tuna, cow cod, ling cod, garibaldi, popeye catalufa, blue rockfish, copper rockfish, vermilion rockfish, sailfish, treefish, yellowtail, albatross, California gull, double-crested cormorant, tufted puffin.**

- In her dream, Pandora saw animals that lived in the distant past. Can you find at least one of each of these animals in the book? The ancient ocean animals are: **Californisaurus, Cymbospondylus, Shonisaurus, Thalattasaur, Hemicalypterus, Leptolepidac, Saurichthys, Semionotus, ammonite, coleoid, lobster.**
The mammals and birds that lived in Yosemite in the past are: **American lion, California tapir, Columbian mammoth, elk, giant sloth, long-horned bison, saber-toothed cat, short-faced bear, Western horse, black-crowned night heron, hoary bat, Roseate spoonbill.**

- You'll probably need to look up some of the animals on the internet to learn what they look like.

Dreaming of